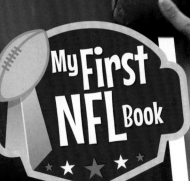

My First **NFL** Book

TENNESSEE TITANS

Steven M. Karras

LET'S READ

AV²
BY WEIGL™

ADDED VALUE • AUDIO VISUAL

Go to **www.av2books.com**, and enter this book's unique code.

BOOK CODE

N 6 4 3 6 6 4

AV² by Weigl brings you media enhanced books that support active learning.

AV² provides enriched content that supplements and complements this book. Weigl's AV² books strive to create inspired learning and engage young minds in a total learning experience.

Your AV² Media Enhanced books come alive with...

 Audio
Listen to sections of the book read aloud.

 Video
Watch informative video clips.

 Embedded Weblinks
Gain additional information for research.

 Try This!
Complete activities and hands-on experiments.

 Key Words
Study vocabulary, and complete a matching word activity.

 Quizzes
Test your knowledge.

 Slide Show
View images and captions, and prepare a presentation.

... and much, much more!

Published by AV² by Weigl
350 5th Avenue, 59th Floor
New York, NY 10118

Website: www.av2books.com

Printed in the United States of America in Brainerd, Minnesota
1 2 3 4 5 6 7 8 9 0 21 20 19 18 17

032017
020317

Editor: Katie Gillespie
Art Director: Terry Paulhus

Weigl acknowledges Getty Images and iStock as the primary image suppliers for this title.

Library of Congress Control Number: 2017930785

ISBN 978-1-4896-5565-3 (hardcover)
ISBN 978-1-4896-5567-7 (multi-user eBook)

My First NFL Book

TENNESSEE TITANS

CONTENTS

2 AV² Book Code
4 Team History
6 The Stadium
8 Team Spirit
10 The Jerseys
12 The Helmet
14 The Coach
16 Player Positions
18 Star Player
19 Famous Player
20 Team Records
22 By the Numbers
24 Quiz/Log on to
    www.av2books.com

3

Team History

The Tennessee Titans' history goes back to 1960. The team was first called the Houston Oilers. The Oilers moved to Tennessee in 1997. They changed their name to the Titans two years later. The Titans have played in one Super Bowl.

The Titans used a trick play called the "Music City Miracle" in 2000. They beat the Buffalo Bills in the last few seconds of the game.

4

NISSAN STADIUM

HOME OF THE TENNESSEE TITANS

1 EAST CONCOURSE

The Stadium

Nissan Stadium is the Titans' home field. It opened in 1999. A store called the Titans Locker Room is open all year. Fans can buy jerseys, hats, and other items there. Nissan Stadium can seat 69,143 people.

Nissan Stadium is on the bank of the Cumberland River in Nashville, Tennessee.

Team Spirit

T-Rac is the Titans' mascot. He is a raccoon. T-Rac wears many outfits during games. He often wears a suit of armor. He also carries a shield and sword with him. T-Rac rides a chariot onto the field. A chariot is a type of wagon pulled by horses.

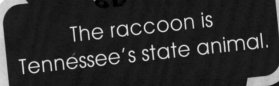

The raccoon is Tennessee's state animal.

The Jerseys

The Titans' main jersey for home games is navy blue. White jerseys are worn at home at the start of the season when it is hot. Wearing darker colors can make players too warm when it is sunny. Both jerseys have light blue on the shoulders. Each sleeve has a picture of a sword shaped like the letter "T."

The Helmet

The Titans wear white helmets with two navy blue stripes down the center. The team logo is on each side. The logo is the letter "T" with three red stars around it in a circle. The circle has blue and red flames on the left side.

The logo has three stars because the Tennessee state flag also has three stars.

WARNING

13

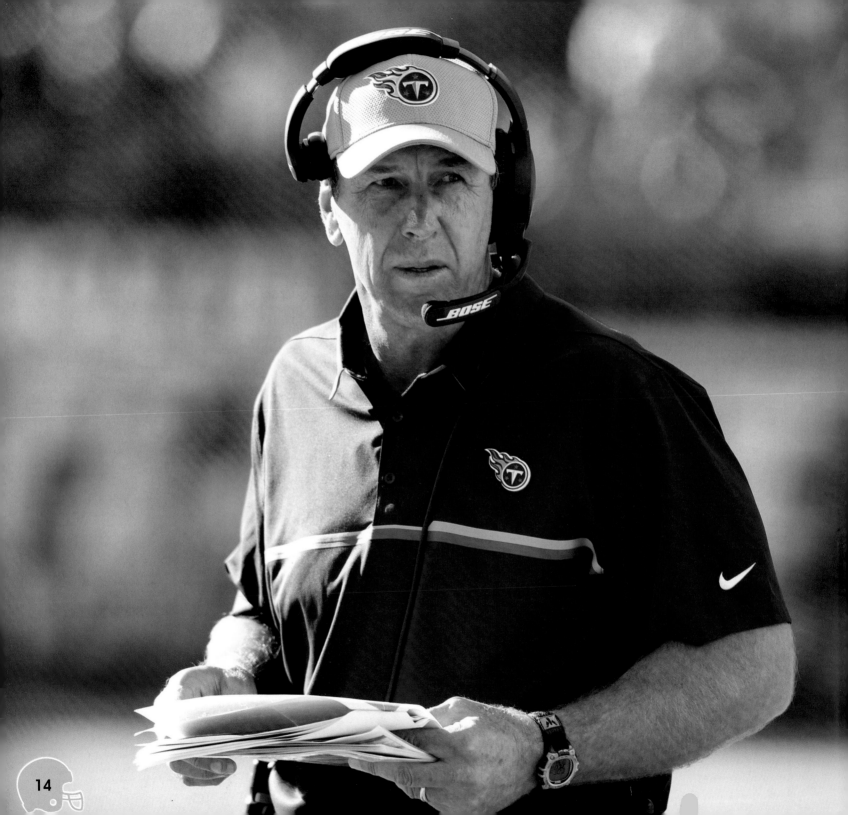

The Coach

Mike Mularkey was hired as the Titans' head coach in 2016. Mularkey played in the NFL for nine seasons. He coached college football before coaching in the NFL. Mularkey was the head coach of two other NFL teams before joining the Titans.

Player Positions

A fullback is an offensive running position. This player lines up next to the running back. The fullback is fast and bigger than the running back. Fullbacks can either help protect the quarterback or run the ball.

Only one fullback has been named the Super Bowl's Most Valuable Player in 50 years.

Marcus Mariota is the Titans' quarterback. He joined the team in 2015. Mariota was given the Heisman Trophy in college. This is the biggest award for college football players. He was the first NFL rookie to throw four touchdown passes in his first regular season game. A rookie is a person playing in his first season.

Eddie George was a running back. He started in every game of his nine seasons with the Titans. George rushed for 10,000 yards in his career. He scored 68 touchdowns. George also played in four Pro Bowls. This is when the best players from each team are invited to play against each other.

Team Records

Quarterback Steve McNair had 76 wins. This is the most of any Titans or Oilers quarterback. Tight end Frank Wycheck led the Titans in receiving yards from 1996 to 2000. Al Del Greco holds the team record for most points scored. He scored 1,060 points in his career.

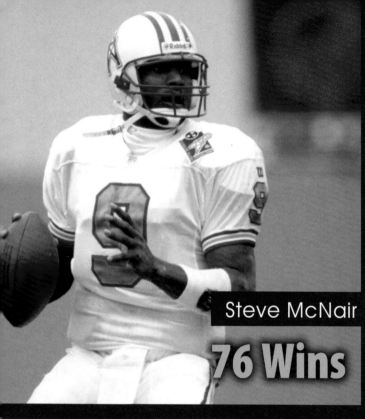

Steve McNair

76 Wins

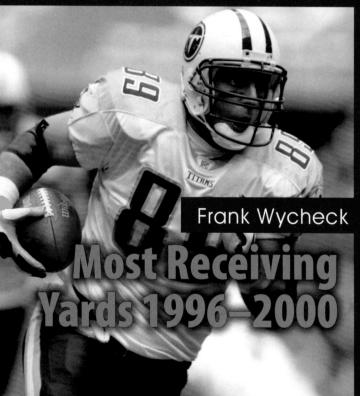

Frank Wycheck

Most Receiving Yards 1996–2000

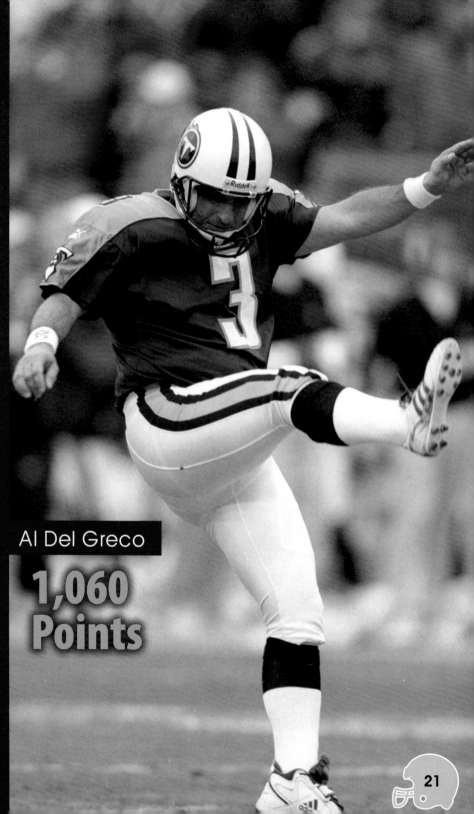

Al Del Greco

1,060 Points

By the Numbers

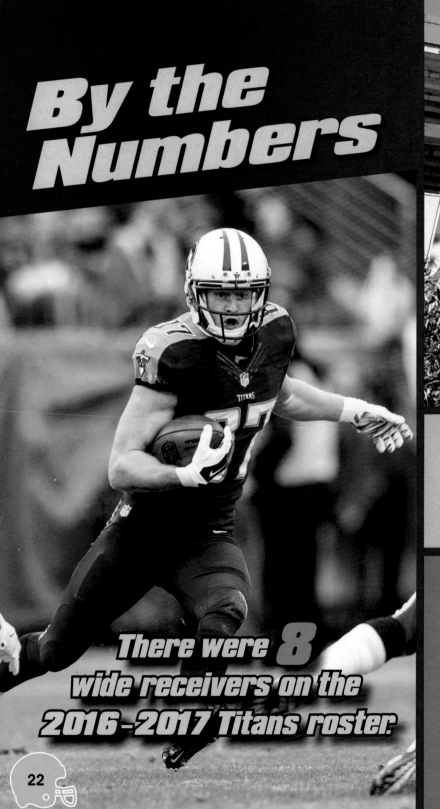

There were **8** wide receivers on the 2016-2017 Titans roster.

The Titans beat the Oakland Raiders **55-0** in 1961.

Ernest Givins caught the ball **542 times** in his career. This is a team record.

Nissan Stadium cost **$290 million** to build.

Mike Mularkey is the Titans' **4th** head coach since the team moved to Tennessee.

The Titans won **13 games** in a row between December 2007 and November 2008.

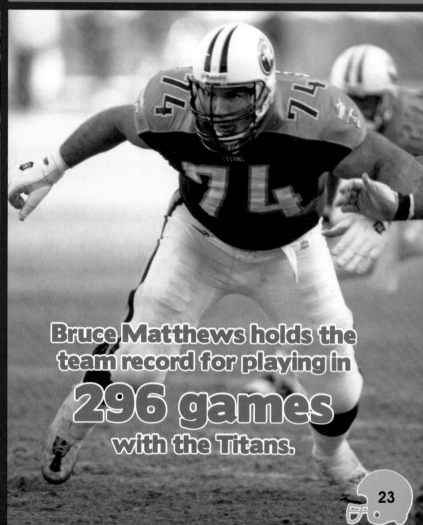

Bruce Matthews holds the team record for playing in **296 games** with the Titans.

Quiz

1. What was the team first called?

2. How many people can Nissan Stadium seat?

3. What is Tennessee's state animal?

4. How many stars are on the Titans' logo?

5. Who holds the team record for most points scored in his career?

Check out www.av2books.com for activities, videos, audio clips, and more!

 Go to www.av2books.com.

 Enter book code. N 6 4 3 6 6 4

Fuel your imagination online!

www.av2books.com

24